**MAGNETS
STUN**

Faraday's Life of Science

Grant Bage

Crosslinks

Series Editors
Grant Bage
Deborah Ramsbotham

First published in 2002
by Anglia Young Books

Reprinted 2005

Anglia Young Books is an imprint of
Mill Publishing Ltd
PO Box 120
Bangor
County Down
BT19 7BX

Illustrations by Robin Lawrie
Design by Angela Ashton

British Library Cataloguing-in-Publication Data

A catalogue record for this book is available from the British Library

ISBN 1 871173 81 7

Printed in Great Britain by Ashford Colour Press, Gosport, Hampshire

CONTENTS PAGE

1
FINDING FARADAY

I am back in the house of my childhood. The
bedroom is dark but not quiet. Rain drums and
patters on the roof-tiles, every window and brick
drips with water. I am lying under thick blankets,
listening, when ... *flash* ... and then ... *crash*. Rain
turns to storm, to thunder and lightning. I can't
sleep now and, as my face presses against the
window, a flicker of light strikes a roof nearby.
Sparks, crackles, splinters: what sort of power is
this lightning, I wonder, as I wriggle back under
the cover?

I used to help Father to tidy the yard, lugging

heavy metal bars to his workshop. Dull slabs of dead iron? Not to me. The metal was dark but not quiet. I noticed small filings of iron sticking to the big bars and some of the larger pieces of iron pushing or pulling away from each other. The iron was talking, though I could not understand what it said. I couldn't understand the lightning, either. I heard adults use words like 'magnet' and 'electricity'. What lies beneath these words?

That was years ago when I was a small boy. Now I am a man – forty years old. My name is Michael Faraday. Perhaps you can picture me, sitting in my favourite chair, reading by the yellow light of a lamp. On the floor is an open box. Scattered around me are scraps of my life so far: notes, letters, lists, diaries, journals. I sift, I read and I smile. Now that I am forty years old, I understand more than that small boy, at least about magnets and electricity. What still puzzles me is 'me'. Why am I so devoted to thinking? Problems, ideas, reasons, explanations, suggestions, questions – they constantly bubble up from inside me. I do not know where that thinking will take me but, in my mind's eye, I see where it started. I hear it too. I imagine myself as a small boy once again, watching my father with wonder:

Clang!

Sparks fizz and fly. Iron notes echo from metal to metal, before dying in the shadows. The blade that father is making dulls from orange to red to grey as the hammer blows shape it.

Clang!

Sparks again, and more sparks. Hammer in hand, my father stands, the hint of a smile gleaming on his soot-soaked face. Is the smile for me, his small son, perched in the corner? Or for the beauty of the metal?

Clang! Father wipes his cheek with the back of his hand and turns. The smile is mine.

Let me tell you more of my family. I was the third child, born on 22nd September 1791 in the smoky city of London. Father was a country blacksmith by trade; Mother was a farmer's daughter. Father's accent was as broad as his shoulders, so thick and north country that Londoners barely understood him. He and my mother had trekked south to London to make a better life for our small family. This they did with faith, my father's tools and many years of hard work.

I try to work hard too, with my own bag of tools. What is in it? From Father I learnt about heating, hammering and looking closely at metals. From church I learnt about the word of God. Add talking, thinking, reading and writing and you have my humble tool-kit. Father shaped his world with a hammer; I try to shape mine with thinking. Father beat metal into beautiful objects – hoes, spades, wheels, chisels, sickles, hooks, hinges; I stretch knowledge into new shapes and sizes. Who knows where that knowledge will lead? Who knows where science may take us?

Will there be candles flickering and spluttering in houses of the future, or could we light the world with a different power? In this year of 1831, steam is already powering railways, where a few years ago there were only horses. Soon the whole country will be criss-crossed with railways and we shall be steaming from London to Glasgow. Or so people tell me. For what man or woman alive can predict what science will achieve? Only this evening, I wrote to my friend Phillips, telling him about my own humble experiments with electricity and magnetism.

23 September 1831   I am busy just now again on Electro-Magnetism and I think I have got hold of a good thing but cannot say; it may be a weed instead of a fish that, after all my labour, I may at last pull up.

You can never tell, with experiments, just where they may lead … but forgive me. Ideas excite my mind, they always have. I am running ahead with my story. I must go back to where it started. I am a small boy once again, in my father's forge.

Clang!

Father's tongs lift and turn the glowing blade as carefully he looks down its length. A final blow, a fizz of sparks and the blade runs straight.

Hiss!

The hot iron plunges into cold water and it is changed. Fire, water, hammer and muscle: Father is moulding metal into objects of beauty. How does it happen? How does the world work?

Difficult questions perhaps, but worth asking. And where better to find answers than in a book?

2
A BOOKISH BOY

You must go to school. That is the law and it is a good law but things used to be different. I was nine years old in the year 1800 and I wanted to go to school more than anything. More than swimming in summer, more than a warm jacket in winter, more than roast beef and steamed plum pudding at Christmas, but how?

Some families paid teachers to stay in their houses, or to visit and give lessons. Families that were rich enough sent their children away for months on end to learn their lessons at boarding schools. My mother and father worked hard, but a blacksmith's wages were counted in copper coins, not gold. After bread, shoes and clothes for a growing family there was little left over to pay for schooling: so I valued each scrap as it came. Every letter, word and idea I chewed over, like my daily bread.

On Sundays we went to our Meeting House and heard words spoken from the Bible. When there was spare time at home, Mother and Father taught us to read from the Bible. If there were any pennies left, we went to day-school. An old teacher and her young helper drilled letters and numbers into my skull, and beat the children who could not remember. It cost a penny a day. If fifty children turned up, that was the size of the class: all ages, all kinds of children, all crowded together. All noise, elbows and smells. I ran there with my friends in the morning, then dawdled and played marbles on the way home.

My church, my parents and the day-school did their best. Even so, I looked back later and wrote about my childhood:

... my education was of the most ordinary description, consisting of little more than the rudiments of reading, writing and

arithmetic at a common day-school. My hours out of school were passed at home and in the streets.

I longed to learn and to read and think but there were no free schools or public libraries to teach people how to learn. The government bought wooden warships to fight the French, not books for blacksmiths' children. I had to find work by the age of twelve and I dreamed of a job with books. Where was a poor blacksmith's son to find such a place?

As luck would have it, it was just around the corner. We lived in west London, off Oxford Street. We had lived in the same small house since I was five years old so I knew those streets like the back of my own hands. I trudged around the local shops, promising a fair day's work for a fair day's pay. That was how I met George Riebau. He liked my manners and he offered me work.

George's shop bulged with things I loved but could never buy: paper, pens, magazines, newspapers and books. At thirteen, I was George's errand boy, fetching paper, carrying books and delivering newspapers. I worked hard and read everything I could. By fourteen, George was teaching me how to bind the pages of books with thread. I became an apprentice bookbinder, signing a promise to work honestly for seven years and learn the trade. I would live in my master's house and obey him like a father.

It was hard work but I had watched my own father in his forge, lending a hand when I could. I soon learnt how to pull, tie and knot fine threads using special bookbinder's tools. The faster I worked with my fingers, the quicker my mind read the pages I tied. What treasures! There were books that told of anything and everything – books called 'encyclopaedias'. In one of these books, I read about electricity: an invisible force that can split tall trees but which crackles softly in silk. This word 'electricity' surged into my own life, as I tried to find out what it was. Other books, like one written by a Swiss woman called Jane Marcet, *talked* about chemistry. In this book, people had conversations but because they were written down on the page, they were easier to understand. Chemistry hinted at a secret world, a hidden knowledge not just of things in my father's forge or the bookbinding shop, but of every single

No. 2
RIEBAU
Blandford St.

material in the world. Little did I know that one day I would meet this clever woman. But that is another story …

With knowledge from George's books and help from my father, I began to build machines. One produced real electricity. By the age of eighteen I was paying for school again, not to learn to read and write, but to hear about science. With a silver shilling, kindly given by my brother when I had no money myself, I paid to hear lectures. In a house just round the corner, at eight o'clock in the evening, a group of us would gather to hear people talk: people like me, fascinated by science but who knew enough to teach it. I was reading, writing, looking and listening: learning was my whole life.

You might be wondering why. Let me tell you. In those days, the streets swarmed with filthy children, begging for a crust here or a penny there. Boys and girls slaved in steaming factories, night after night, and slept five-in-a-bed during the day. On Sundays, crowds ambled along to watch people being punished for stealing. Families would chat or hoot in amusement, watching as the rope was wound around a slender young neck. Streaming tears, a mumbled prayer and *snap*: another dead thief, one more useless body, swinging in the wind.

God and learning could help us make better lives than that. I tried to explain this to my little sister, Margaret. She was the baby of our family, born when I was eleven. I helped to look after her, playing with her at home or taking her out in the streets, and I loved her dearly. At the age of twenty-three, I had to go abroad for the first time. My father had died a few years before, leaving my mother alone. I did not see Mother or my little sister for nearly two years, so I wrote as many letters as I could. Here is one of them:

Rome

29 December 1814

Dear Margaret,

I am very happy to hear that you got my last letter, and I am as happy to say that I have received yours ... Give my love with a kiss to Mother, the first thing you do on reading the letter, and tell her how much I think on her and you. I hope that all your friends are well.

I am also pleased to hear that you go to school, and I hope that you have enough to do there. Your writing is not improved quite so much in one year as I expected but ... it is pretty well ... For my questions about Rome and Naples look into some book at school, or at Mr Riebau's or elsewhere. I hope you do not neglect your figures ... they are almost as necessary as writing. Of French you say nothing, but I suppose you still work at it.

I must now, dear Margaret, put an end to this letter. Give my warmest love to Mother and to Robert, Betsy, Mr Gray and the little ones, and all your friends. Write again, at an opportunity, to your affectionate brother.

Michael Faraday.

All my life I have been trying to catch up with people who had a better education than I.

I wanted to make myself into a learned man. To do this I needed help, just as my little sister Margaret needed help from me. The person who helped me most, who really believed in me, was my close friend, Ben. Let me tell you about him – about our letters – and about how we learnt to think differently.

3
LEARNING LIFE

I have been lucky in my life so far and I thank God
for it. But I know that somehow I am *different*. I
seem to see the world in different ways from most
people. I cannot quite tell whether I was born that
way or whether I taught myself. For example, one
of my best friends was Benjamin Abbott, a lively
lad two years younger than I. After a rough sort of
schooling, both of us earned our living at jobs that
had nothing to do with science. Ben was a clerk in
the City of London, scribbling away in an office at
letters and sums. I worked in the bookbinding
shop, trying hard to read books between making,
delivering or selling them for other people. What
little spare money we had, we spent on joining

scientific clubs or paying to hear lectures. We did dream and joke about growing rich, becoming famous and marrying the prettiest women in London, but the truth is that we were even busier thinking and writing.

We wrote countless letters to each other, which we have kept as a sign of our friendship. When I read them again now – what fun and nonsense! In one letter (scribbled in July 1812, when I was twenty years old) I wrote hundreds of words telling Ben a ridiculous story about my walk home from seeing him the day before. It was pouring with summer rain but I was so excited about the science we had been discussing that I simply saw science in everything. Puffed out and panting, I stood in the middle of a puddle and I began to wonder how our bodies can feel cool on the inside, while making so much heat that they steam on the outside. Then I started thinking about why raindrops do not pass through human skin, though that skin is thin and fragile and the rain is dropping so fast from the sky. There was lots more nonsense like this, too much and too silly to bore you with now.

My sisters tease me, saying that I have

always had my head in the clouds or my nose in a book. In one of my other letters to Ben, I showed that this was not fair. For in it I described how my head had been trapped between railings, then banged with a door. It sounds strange but it is true, so let me tell you the story of how it happened. Ben and I had been trying to work out whether our thoughts came from inside our heads, or whether thoughts could begin in another part of the body, or begin outside the body, or begin nowhere at all! Young people often like to work out odd things like this, though most adults are too busy being dull to give them a moment's thought. Anyway, Ben and I were writing to each other about this when I recounted something that had happened a few years before:

2 August 1812

Dear Abbott,

Didn't I promise you a proof that ideas were formed in the head? It is hardly worth having but as it costs nothing, take it. Six or seven years ago, when I was about fourteen, I was standing at the door of a gentleman's house at which I was delivering some books. Whilst waiting for my knock on the door to be answered, I thrust my head through some iron railings that separated his house from next door. Then I began to think: my head is on one side of the rails and my body is on the other. Which side am I on? I had just made up my mind in favour of this being the side my head was upon, since it was my head that contained most of my senses, when I was brought back to earth with a bump. The front door of the neighbouring house was swung open upon my nose, so hard that it began to bleed and all thinking stopped immediately. Simple as this proof is, it seems as strong as any other I have heard since ...

Yours sincerely,
Faraday

Perhaps it was right that I ended up a scientist, for as you can see I was not very good at delivering books! That is how God worked things out for me. One day I was a humble bookbinder, paying to hear lectures and writing foolish letters to my friends. The next day … well, let me tell you about those next days and how my fortune was made.

4
FARADAY TRAVELS TO FOREIGN LANDS

Do you know what magnets do? They can draw metals forwards or push them away. Magnetic power is invisible: we only know it is there because it moves things.

In my life, there have been people like that. George Riebau, one of the kindest men ever, drew me to books. In his shop, books then drew me to science. After that, I had a turn of luck. Writing careful notes at a lecture helped me not just to read about science, but to travel all over Europe, to work as a scientist and to make my fortune. This is how it happened.

Seven years I worked for George, binding

pages into books. In my spare time I read, made machines and listened to clever people discussing science. Yet how could I remember it all? I kept science notebooks, crammed with scribbles and drawings. After handing over my silver shilling, I would listen to a lecture and try to write everything down. This was hard on my wrist. My handwriting scrawled like a spider and the ideas became muddled. George put me right.

"Just note down a name for each different part of the talk," he said, gently. "Then, when you come through that back door, sit straight down at the table and write down everything you remember."

Soon my notes and booklets were so clear that George started showing them to customers buying science books in the shop. One gentleman liked my writing and gave me a free ticket for some lectures by the famous scientist, Sir Humphry Davy. I went, listened and wrote my notes in the usual way. Feeling bolder than ever before in my life, I sent Sir Humphry my notebook. I had written down his words and ideas carefully: might Sir Humphry be able to find me a job, enquiring into science?

The next morning a servant, dressed in a fine green coat with silver buttons, brought a note to the shop. It was from Sir Humphry: this could change my life! My palms sweated with fear as I slit open the envelope. "I am obliged to go out of town and shall not be returned for a month." That was not the answer I hoped for.

You may not believe in God: I do. Was God at work in what happened next? Soon after, Sir Humphry was peering closely into a glass jar, filled with gas. With no warning, the glass cracked and shattered. *Bang!* Sir Humphry's eye needed a patch and ointment. That is where I came in. He remembered my notebooks: their neatness, the accurate drawings, how I seemed to have understood his ideas.

"Send for that young fellow Faraday," he ordered his servant. "I cannot see and I cannot write, with this damned wound in my eye. But I think I know a young man who might do that for me."

I worked for Sir Humphry briefly, until his eye healed, and then I had to go back to my bookbinding. Then Sir Humphry's laboratory assistant (a young lad named William Payne) was dismissed, for fighting at work. Sir Humphry offered me the job instead. My wages would be twenty-five shillings a week and I would live in two rooms at the top of the house.

The rest is history. Within a few days I had given up bookbinding. Within a few months, I was travelling around Europe with Sir Humphry and Lady Davy. I became his trusted assistant, visiting some of the finest scientists and museums in France, Italy and Switzerland.

However, until this time, I had never been more than twelve miles outside London! This first trip abroad filled me with fear and hope. It was especially exciting because France, the first country we visited, was at war with England. We needed special passports. We had to promise not to spy or make trouble, and swear that our only interest was science. Newspapers in England did not understand and printed that Sir Humphry was doing a bad thing by visiting France, 'the enemy of his country'. It did not seem bad to me!

All of a sudden, my job, my journey and my life seemed thrilling. I wanted to remember it all so I wrote a daily journal. It finished up as a book of nearly two hundred pages, describing all the

interesting things that I saw. As I read those pages again, the sheer excitement of travel floods back into my mind:

30 December 1813   Though seen only by the faintness of starlight yet I am sure our road was beautiful, along the bank of a river and within a few yards of the water which indeed at times came to the horses' feet. On our left was a series of small hills and valleys lightly wooded ... It is pleasant to state out loud to the mind, the newness of all this ... The French River Loire is on my right hand. The houses to the left contain men of another country to myself. It is French ground I am passing over ... We seem tied to no spot ... We move with freedom, our world is extending and existence enlarged ... We seem to fly over the globe.

This land may have been full of my own nation's enemies, but everything was interesting and so much of it was new. In Paris I noticed how cleverly the streets were lit:

2 December 1813   Lighting in the streets in Paris is very good. They use large lamps placed at a distance from each other and high up in the air over the middle of the street ... It seems dangerous, though I must say I never heard of an accident. A strong rope is stretched across the street to which another is tied near the middle. This runs first through a pulley to which the lamp is attached and then through another pulley fixed to the first rope. Afterwards it passes to the side of the house and then over another pulley, down the wall to a little box constantly locked, of which the lamplighter has the key. The lamp has two large burners and three reflectors, one behind each burner and the other over them, throwing the light in useful directions.

My travels with Sir Humphry were not all wonderful: in 1814, I saw cruelty too. In Italy, a man was hung up by his arms as a punishment for throwing mud at soldiers. Two soldiers had a fight in the street where we were staying, stabbing each other in the stomach with long knives. On one occasion, I too felt that I was stabbed in the back, though luckily not with a real knife and without lasting damage. An injury to my pride was inflicted by a so-called 'noble woman'. Worse still, she was married to my master, Sir Humphry.

Sir Humphry was a clever scientist and I was his scientific helper. Sir Humphry was also an English gentleman. He wore fine clothes, ate large meals and loved nothing more than shooting birds and catching fish. For this he needed another sort of helper: a servant. Unluckily for me, the servant whom Sir Humphry had planned to take to Europe refused to come at the last minute. His wife thought it was too dangerous to travel abroad: remember, British and French soldiers were still killing each other in the war.

So it was me, the young and nervous Michael Faraday, who ended up doing both jobs: scientist and servant to Sir Humphry. I did not just have experiments to set up, equipment to clean and notes to make, but meals to organise, bills to pay and other servants to command. None of this was work that I was used to. To make matters worse, I had, it seemed, made an enemy in my own camp.

'Proud' and 'haughty' are words we rarely use in science. These were the words I wrote in my journal though, to describe Sir Humphry's wife. Lady Davy was a spiteful woman, who always wished to have her own way. We had many arguments, some of which I won, but there was one argument that I lost. I have hardly spoken to anybody about it since it happened and I could not bear to recount it in my journal. But I shall tell you about it now.

We had reached Switzerland, a land of mountains and also many scientists. Sir Humphry had arranged for us to meet two of them, Jane and Alexander Marcet. Jane Marcet wrote one of the best books I ever read about science, called

Conversations on Chemistry. I discovered it first in the bookshop where I used to work: now I was to meet its author!

As you know, I am a plain man whose father was a blacksmith. Dinner parties in smart clothes make me nervous but I have always had good manners and a quick mind. So when Sir Humphry mentioned that I could go with him to dine at the Marcet household, I could not wait to meet my heroine, Jane. We were shown into the house. The ladies and gentlemen were seated for drinks. Then the bell rang for dinner. Jane Marcet led the way to the dining room, but before I could follow her, Lady Davy turned to me. In a sharp, loud voice, she said the cruellest thing:

"Mr Faraday, you will now go and eat your meal in the kitchen, with the rest of the *servants*."

I was speechless and powerless. My one chance to talk with this famous and inspiring woman had been snatched away by another woman who saw no difference between a scientist and a servant.

Envy, money and manners: there are more invisible powers shaping our lives than science can measure. So let me tell you about another

huge power that I *was* able to observe, with care, as a scientist should: the volcano of Mount Vesuvius.

5
ON THE EDGE

Our journey across Europe took us to many places to meet many people but little did I know, when I sailed away from England, that one stop would be Mount Vesuvius. In case you don't know, Mount Vesuvius is a volcano in Italy – an active volcano. With one shudder or shake, this wonder of nature can crush, swallow or poison a person, as thoughtlessly as you or I might swat a fly. It is not a place for feeble or weak-hearted visitors, but it is a place for scientists. Sir Humphry and I were drawn towards the mountain not just for the thrill of climbing it, but also for the thrill of understanding it. What could we learn for science through observing the summit of this volcano?

Mount Vesuvius erupts rarely, so its lower slopes are dotted with farms and fields growing grapes, figs and other fruit in the rich soil. Half-way up the mountain there is even an inn where visitors can rest and eat before they take the stony road to the top.

The summit is changing all the time. Sometimes it grows as more ashes are thrown out; sometimes it shrinks when eruptions blast away the very ground itself. Climbing the mountain was some of the hardest exercise I have ever done, for there is no clear path and the ground is covered with rocks and boulders. Streams and streams of lava have boiled over from the inside of the volcano and run down its slopes in different directions. This lava is cold now and set hard but it is so thickly covered with dust and stones that a climber's feet scrabble and slip one pace back for every two he goes forward. The climb was worth it though, as I wrote in my journal:

13 May 1814   By the aid of sticks and two or three restings, we attained the top by about half-past two o'clock. Here the volume of smoke and flame appeared immense and the scene was fearfully grand. The ground beneath us was very hot and smoke and vapour issued out from various spots around us.

On the top of the summit rises a small mountain, which from a distance appears covered with sulphur. This we climbed, and then came to a resting-place, from where the mouth of the volcano and part of the crater were visible. From here we had a fine view of the fire. The wind was kind and blew the smoke from us, and at times we could see the flames breaking out with extraordinary force, and the smoke and vapour ascending in enormous clouds; and when silence was made, the roaring of the flames came fearfully over the ear.

We then advanced to a piece of ground thrown up on the edge of the crater, and *were then within 100 feet of the orifice from where the flames were coming. Here we had a fine view of the crater, appearing as an enormous funnel, and the smoke billowing out in abundance from most parts of it. It was encrusted in many places with the same yellow substance we had observed before, and which Sir Humphry said was 'iron chloride'.*

After standing there for a few minutes, we suddenly had to move back swiftly, as the wind changed direction and blew poisonous sulphur smoke and gas towards us. Rather dangerously, I stayed for a few moments longer to collect some soil samples, and then had to dart back to avoid being caught in the strong-smelling cloud. That night I wrote up my scientific observations in my journal:

There appeared to be two distinct types of smoke or vapour.

That which came from the mouth of the volcano was very dense, or a yellow-white colour, and rolled away like clouds in the sky. Judging from the odour blown to us by the wind, it appeared to consist mostly of sulphurous acid gas and water.

From other places a white vapour arose which disappeared rapidly as steam would do ... On the spot where we were, a great heat was evident, and in cavities in the lava it was too strong for the hand to bear. A boy who came up with us cooked some eggs by this heat, and laid them out with bread and wine as a snack ...

We were so fascinated by the power of the volcano that we decided to risk another visit the next day. This time it took us until half past seven in the evening to climb to the top. In the gathering darkness, the volcano was even more spectacular:

14 May 1814   It now became dark very quickly, and the flames appeared more and more awful – at one time enclosed in the smoke, and everything hid from our eyes; and then the flames flashing upwards and lighting through the cloud, till by a turn of the wind the orifice was cleared, and the dreadful place appeared uncovered and in all its horrors. The flames then issued forth in whirlwinds, and rose many yards above the mouth of the volcano. The flames were of a light red colour, and at one time, when I had the best view of the mouth, appeared to issue from an orifice about three yards or more long.

When I read my journal again now, the climb sounds dangerous. I suppose it would have been if the mountain had decided to erupt at that moment. Yet that did not stop us having a party on top of the volcano to celebrate our second climb to the summit. Bread, chicken, turkey, wine, water and eggs, roasted on the hot rocks, were laid out on the flattest piece of ground we could find. Everyone ate and drank to their heart's content. Afterwards we raised our glasses to drink the health of England, then sang in lusty voices 'God Save The King' and 'Rule, Britannia'.

I was twenty-three years old and the son of a poor blacksmith; I had not even been to a proper school. Yet here I was, over a thousand miles from home, eating a picnic on top of Europe's best-known volcano, working with England's most famous scientist. My head swam with excitement and my eyes stung, not just with sulphur and smoke but with tears of homesickness. Tears for my beloved father, who had died four years earlier, and for my mother, sisters and brother back in London. If they could see me now, how proud they would be …

6
DREAMING ... OF QUESTIONS

I started thinking about all these stories when I reached for that box of papers. How long have I been sitting here, dreaming? It must be hours but here I am, still in my favourite chair, reading by the yellow light of the lamp. On the floor is the open box and scattered around are these scraps of my life: notes, letters, lists, diaries, journals.

I was forty years old yesterday and I have been dreaming and questioning all my life: 'Why are you doing that, Father?' 'What does this book tell me about electricity?' 'Could we think about it another way?' I have been asking questions all my life – and writing down the answers. When I was in Italy with Sir Humphry, for instance, I told my journal how we found a fish that generates electricity. But where did that electricity come from?

These strange fish are called 'torpedoes' because they stun their enemies with electric shocks. Three torpedoes had been caught in the local lake and an Italian scientist kept them in a bucket for us to examine. We put some tin plates on to one fish and joined wires to the plates. Would electricity come through these plates and wires? Might it be strong enough to shock our fingers, or even heat the water? I felt nothing when I tried, though Sir Humphry claimed his fingertips tingled. We decided that the fish were too tired and the weather too cold for a proper experiment. Luckily the next day, somebody brought us a bigger specimen to look at. Unluckily, it was dead. We slit open the scaly flesh to investigate how a fish could make electricity. As the strong smell from its belly filled the air, we peered inside and saw that a quarter of the body was stuffed with tubes, oozing a pale, clear jelly. These tubes were close to the head of the fish and it was from the head that the electric shocks came. Did the tubes and the jelly together make the electricity? It seemed like a good idea. Sir Humphry tested the fish and found that the whole body could conduct electricity. The jelly in the tubes tested strongly positive but we could go no further with the experiment. We had run out of time – and torpedoes. The secret of the shocking fish was safe, for now.

We had not run out of things to look at. A few days later we travelled to the Italian city of Florence, where I had an experience that I will never forget. We were shown round a museum and, as we passed through one of the rooms, I picked up an old telescope. Why was it here? It did not look special. Then the people at the museum told me who had made it. It was Galileo's telescope: Galileo was one of the first and finest scientists the world has ever known. Were it not for the fact that it was recorded in my journal, in my own scrawling handwriting, I would scarcely believe it myself:

21 March 1814   In one place was Galileo's first telescope, that with which he discovered Jupiter's satellites. It was a simple tube of wood and paper about three and a half feet long with a lens at each end, the field of view was very small. Here was also the first lens which Galileo made; it was set in a very pretty frame of brass with an inscription in Latin on it. The lens itself is cracked across.

As I held this tube – a tube that changed how people thought about the universe – I smiled, thinking back to the machines I had built as a boy, trying to make electricity. This museum was full of machines far more powerful than my own childish efforts. Somebody, somewhere in the past had made a battery so strong that its discharge had burnt a hole straight through a thick glass jar without shattering the rest of the glass. The jar was so strong that not even a hammer could smash it. I held that jar in my hands too and as my fingers played around the melted glass, I mused about the power in that battery.

Writing in my journal kept such memories fresh, but I realised, as I held that jar, that this dusty museum did the same. In this building, I could *see* how people had thought about science, for hundreds of years. I could *touch* what they had touched and try what they had tried. Looking at these old things brought dead thoughts back to life.

Not that the museum was just about the past. Its rooms contained precious scientific equipment and we soon designed an exciting experiment. What would happen if we … tried to burn a diamond? Diamonds are so rare that rich people wear them in rings. Diamonds are so hard that they can cut through glass, metal and even other stones. But could diamonds be burnt, through the power of the sun? That was something else we tried in Italy, with the Grand Duke of Tuscany's 'burning glass'. I had come across a 'burning glass' before, as many children have. I remember, as a nine-year-old in London, playing with my family's precious magnifying glass and being told off by my mother for leaving it out in the yard. My brother had held up the glass on a summer's day, tilting it this way and that until the sun's rays centred in a single, bright beam. I watched, fascinated, as the dry grass under the beam smouldered, smoked and burst into flames. Then I played with the glass for hours by myself, enthralled by the power in that bright spot of light.

What we tried in Italy was not so different from those childhood games in our back yard in London. True, the Grand Duke of Tuscany's glass was bigger and in Italy we also designed our fun as a scientific experiment: we planned carefully, looked carefully, recorded carefully and thought carefully about everything that happened. We tried to predict what might happen. But the excitement – well, that was just the same as in the game. Could we do something that had never been done? Even better, could we try and explain it? The words I wrote in my journal bring the memories flooding back:

27 March 1814   Today we made the grand experiment of burning the diamond and the things seen were beautiful and interesting. A small glass globe was emptied of air and filled with pure oxygen gas. The diamond was supported in the centre of this globe by a rod, to the top of which a cradle or cup was fixed. This was pierced full of holes to allow a free circulation of the gas about the diamond.

The Duke's burning glass was used to apply heat to the diamond. It consists of two double convex lenses distant from each other by about 4 feet. The large lens is about 14 or 15 inches in diameter, the small one about 3 inches in diameter. The instrument is fixed in the centre of a round table and can be pointed up or down.

The instrument was placed in the upper room of the museum and having arranged it at the window the diamond was placed in the focus and anxiously watched. The heat was continued at intervals for $^3/_4$ of an hour (it being necessary to cool the globe at times) and during that time it was thought that the

diamond was slowly diminishing and becoming opaque.

On a sudden Sir H. Davy observed the diamond to burn visibly and when removed from the focus it was found to be in a state of active and rapid combustion. The diamond glowed brilliantly with a scarlet light inclining to purple and when placed in the dark continued to burn for about four minutes. After cooling the glass, heat was again applied to the diamond and it burned again though not nearly so long as before. This was repeated twice more and soon after the diamond became all consumed. This phenomenon, of actual and vivid combustion has never been observed before ... The globe and contents were put bye for future examination.

'Put bye for future examination'. I cannot recall exactly the ideas that the 'globe and contents' led to, for it was many years ago and much has happened since. Then, I was a young man with nothing, on his first visit to Europe. Now I live in my own house, I work as a scientist, I write books and I am married. Might I even have discovered, in these last few weeks, how to use magnetism to *make* electricity?

Smiling, I flick through the journal that travelled with me to Europe. The pages have faded and curled a little, but it has done its job. It has given me *words,* which I have 'put bye for future examination'. One day perhaps other people may read my journal too for, without meaning to, I seem to have become quite famous. If they happen to read my words in a future I cannot see, I would ask them only to remember this:

I was a humble blacksmith's son, who never learnt science at school. With God's help I have changed the world, a little. And I have done it through dreaming ... of questions.

THE LIFE OF MICHAEL FARADAY

Michael Faraday was one of the best scientists of the Victorian age. His experiments led to discoveries that still help us today, especially in understanding electricity and magnetism. Modern technology like dynamos and electric motors are possible because of his work. However, fame did not seem to affect Faraday. Most writers say that he was a kind, modest and religious man.

We know little about Faraday's early life. He was born in London in 1791 and his father, James, was a blacksmith. For seven years, until he was twenty-one, Faraday worked as an apprentice bookbinder, going to scientific clubs and lectures in his spare time. Between 1813 and 1815 he travelled around Europe with a famous scientist called Sir Humphry Davy.

Faraday returned home to a job in the best laboratory in Britain, at the Royal Institution. 1821 was a big year for Faraday: he was promoted at work, married Sarah Barnard, and made a public promise at his church to keep his faith. In September 1821, in the basement laboratory at the Royal Institution, he did some experiments that helped him discover 'electromagnetic rotation'. This is the main idea behind the electric motor.

In the next few years, Faraday experimented with chemicals like chlorine and benzine, and on making glass for lenses. Faraday was also interested in teaching science. In 1826 he started the 'Friday Evening Discourses' (public talks and demonstrations) and invented the Royal Institution 'Christmas Lectures' for children. These lectures still take place today and are broadcast on television. In 1831 Faraday did more experiments on electromagnetism and discovered 'electromagnetic induction', the principal idea behind electric transformers and generators. Without this discovery, electricity would not be the power that it is today.

From 1836, Faraday worked on improving lighthouses. In the 1840s he designed a better chimney for oil-burning lamps. This technology was installed in all lighthouses and also at Buckingham Palace. By the early 1860s, Faraday was trying to power lighthouses with electricity. He also helped to improve safety in coal mines, advised the Army and Navy, researched light, electromagnetism and chemicals, and became a leader in his church. After all this hard work, Faraday had a breakdown.

By 1858 Faraday was a frail but famous man. Queen Victoria gave him a house to live in. Faraday started to take things more easily, though he still worked hard for his church. He died on 25 August 1867 and was buried in Highgate Cemetery.